Jesus' 12 Disciples

Matthew 10:2-4; Luke 6:13-16 FOR CHILDREN

Written by Louise Ulmer
Illustrated by Art Kirchhoff

ARCH® Books

Copyright © 1982 CONCORDIA PUBLISHING HOUSE
ST. LOUIS, MISSOURI
MANUFACTURED IN THE UNITED STATES OF AMERICA
ALL RIGHTS RESERVED
ISBN 0-570-06160-1

One day when the world was dark with sin
Jesus said, "It is time to begin.
My Father in heaven has a job I must do.
I will work day and night until I am through.
I must show the world a new way to live.
It will take every moment I can give.
I need some good men to work with Me.
They will help change the world
        and make people free."

Wherever He went Jesus started to preach.
Great crowds gathered round to hear Him teach.
He was such a great teacher that when word got 'round
    rich men and poor came and sat on the ground.
By dozens and hundreds the people came,
    even the sick, the blind, and the lame.
His news was more joyful than any could tell;
    they came to Christ sick, but they went away well.

A man named Andrew sat there with another.
He got so excited he ran home for his brother.
They listened to all Jesus had to say
  as He told them to live in a brand-new way.

"Peter," said Andrew, "do you think we can
be good and kind to every man?"

"I think," said Peter, "we surely should try.
If Jesus says, 'Do it,' on Him we'll rely.
He says it's the way God wants us to be,
and Jesus' word is enough for me."

So Peter and Andrew told every friend.
They talked about Jesus again and again.
"Let's try to do everything Jesus would do,"
    said Peter the fisherman to brother Andrew.

James and John, sons of Zebedee,
    were fishermen too on Lake Galilee.
James was older. His hair was gray,
    but he kept on fishing day after day.
John was a strong boy, brave and true,
    with a smile and a song the whole day through.

To Galilee's shore one day Jesus came
  to watch Peter, Andrew, John, and James.
As He watched them fishing in the blistering sun,
  He was full of love for every one.

"Come, follow Me!" He called to the four;
  and they left their fishing boats docked on the shore.

Said Jesus:

"Fishers of men you will be for Me,
    and the light of the world, so people can see.
I came here to die for this world full of strife,
    so that all of its people can have a new life.
Fight the good fight. Run the good race.
Together we'll tell the world of God's grace."

A few days later in a dusty town
    another man laid his business down.
Matthew, the tax collector, followed the Lord.
He left his money without a word.

Said Jesus:

"Treasures in heaven I'll give to you,
    when all our work on earth is through.
In heaven silver and gold cannot rust,
    but the treasures of earth will turn to dust."

Thomas heard Jesus preach Good News to the poor.
He wanted to follow, but He couldn't be sure.
"If this Man is from God, I will give Him my life."
Thomas said one day to his gentle wife.
"Jesus must be God's Son to know God so well.
The things He knows no man could tell.
Jesus heals broken hearts and sets men free.
He turned water to wine. He walked on the sea.
I guess that is proof enough for me."

Philip's family were both Greeks and Jews.
He could speak either language he happened to choose.
Philip heard about Jesus and spread the good news.
"Come with Me," Jesus said, "You're a man I can use."

"I must go get Nathanael, my best friend.
He will want to come with us," Philip grinned.
Nathanael Bartholomew sat by a fig tree
        when Philip called him to come and see.

"I've found the Messiah, the King of the Jews.
He wants us to work with Him preaching the news."
Bartholomew came to where Jesus sat preaching.
Jesus looked up with the folks He was teaching.

"Nathanael," He said, "I already know you.
You're a man who is honest through and through.
I saw you before sitting under the fig tree.
Will you leave your job and come with Me?"

"How can He know what I think and say?
How can He see my tree far away?
Only God could see my heart this way."
Nathanael Bartholomew smiled, "Yes, Lord.
I'll follow You always. I give You my word."

Peter and Andrew, fishers of men,
　　followed Jesus to the end.
Nathanael Bartholomew, Philip his friend,
　　two more good men for Jesus to send.
Sons of Thunder were John and James,
Fiery men with highest aims.
In the kingdom of heaven they tried to be best.
Jesus taught them the greatest must serve all the rest.

Simon the Zealot! Who would have guessed
    that Jesus would pick such a man from the rest?
Zealots were rebels who fought and spied.
To get rid of the Romans they killed and lied.
Jesus saw something else when He looked at Simon.
Simon's outside was rough, but inside was a diamond.

Judas, son of James, and Little James—
    we don't know much more than these men's names.
These two disciples must have been shy;
    they didn't talk much, but we don't know why.
They listened to everything Jesus would say,
    and they worked for the Master night and day.

Eleven good men but one was not.
His name was Judas Iscariot.
Poor Judas, what was it that happened to you?
You didn't love Jesus enough to be true.

Peter, Andrew, James, and John
    followed Jesus on and on.
Matthew, Thomas, Philip too;
    don't forget Bartholomew.
Simon, Judas, and Little James
    are eleven of the apostles' names.
Eleven good men and one that was not;
    his name was Judas Iscariot.

They lived with the Master three short years.
They shared His laughter and sadness and tears.
Sometimes they were foolish; sometimes they did wrong.
Sometimes they were weak; sometimes they were strong.

And when Jesus' time on earth was through,
He left them a very great job to do.
Now this job is for me and for you.

Said Jesus:
"Fishers of men you will be for Me,
      and the light of the world, so people can see.
Fight the good fight. Run the good race.
Together we'll tell the world of God's grace."

DEAR PARENTS:

Very early in His ministry, Jesus selected and trained 12 ordinary men to help Him—and eventually succeed Him—in the extraordinary task of preaching the Gospel of forgiveness and eternal life to all people.

This small book recounts how each of these 12 apostles was called individually and personally by our Lord. Your children might wish that they could have been there, that they could have been called personally by Jesus, too.

Tell them they were! While they are not apostles like Peter, James, or John, they have been individually called to be Christ's special disciples. That happened at their baptism. There they died and rose again with Jesus (Romans 6:3-5), and there the risen Christ called them by name and made them a special part of everything His death and resurrection had accomplished.

Your child's baptism may have seemed like a very ordinary moment in the life of your church. It wasn't. It had extraordinary, everlasting results.

THE EDITOR